PERFECT GUIDE ARCHERY FOR BEGINNERS

Learn A to Z about Archery, aim and shoot that Target accurately with ease

STEFAN MILLER

Table of Contents

INTRODUCTION 4

CHAPTER 1 7

    COMMON TYPES OF BOWS 7

    OLYMPIC RECURVE 7

    COMPOUND BOW 9

    TRADITIONAL BOWS 12

    WHY WOULD YOU WANT TO SHOOT A RECURVE BOW 15

    WHAT SIZE LONGBOW DO I NEED? 16

    LONGBOW STRINGING TECHNIQUES 16

        HOW TO SHOOT A LONGBOW 17

    RECURVE BOW SHOOTING TECHNIQUES 21

    RECURVE OR LONGBOW: WHICH IS SUPERIOR? 26

CHAPTER 2 28

    ARCHERY KIT 28

    SUPPLIES ONE WILL NEED TO START ARCHERY 28

    ACCESSORIES AND OTHER TOOLS 31

    THE BASICS PARTS OF A BOW: 32

    5 MAIN TYPES OF ARCHERY 37

CHAPTER 3 44

    EYE DOMINANCE 44

    PROPER SHOOTING FORM 45

    ARCHERY LESSONS AND PROGRAMS FOR NEW ARCHERS 51

- FUN WAYS TO ENJOY YOUR BOW 55
- OUR BOW RECOMMENDATIONS FOR NEW ARCHERS 59
- HOW TO MEASURE FOR THE RIGHT-SIZED BOW FOR YOU 65
- BOW PACKAGES AND ADDITIONAL EQUIPMENT 68
- BOW RELEASES AND/OR TABS 70
- ARROWS MADE OF ALUMINUM 75
- ARROWS MADE OF CARBON 75
- WOODEN ARROWS 75
- HOW TO PURCHASE A BOW 79
- ARROW BUYERS GUIDE 80
- ARROW SHAFT COMPONENTS 80
- SELECT THE PROPER ARROWHEADS 85
- WHERE TO BUY BOW AND ARROWS 87

CHAPTER 4 89
- SOME BASIC RULES YOU SHOULD KNOW ABOUT ARCHERY 89
- TIPS FOR ALL ARCHERS ON HOW TO PICK A BOW SIGHT 91
- COMPARISON OF SINGLE AND MULTI-PIN SIGHTS 92
- SIZE OF PINS 96
- FIBER OPTICS 97
- SIGHT LIGHTS 98
- BUBBLE LEVELS 99
- GANG ADJUSTMENTS 99

INTRODUCTION

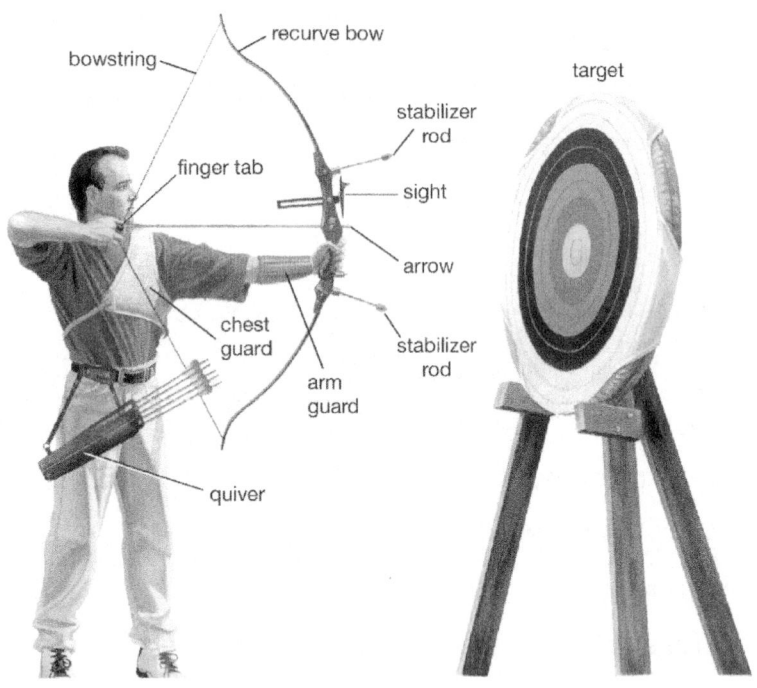

To even try out several sports, one must make significant upfront investments. However, releasing your first arrow is simple. You can try and enjoy a sport that draws people for life by making a quick phone call to an archery shop in your area.

The best places to learn about archery, get your equipment fixed, and get started are in archery shops.

Most stores give instruction. If they don't, their professional can suggest an instructor for you.

It's crucial to establish a relationship with a store. Your go-to sources for all things archery are the store's experts. Online "great discounts" are alluring, but be careful what you wish for. A bow cannot be pulled out of its box and used for immediate shooting. To configure it to fit you, you need an expert.

With a fast internet search, you may locate a nearby archery store. Ask about lessons and activities at the first store you come across. You can rent bows from several stores to use for lessons. That's a fantastic method to learn the sport without diving in and purchasing equipment.

You'll discover a teacher who is eager to help when you go to your first lesson. While learning the fundamentals of archery, you'll shoot your first arrows at close range. Your accuracy will improve and you'll be able to shoot farther as your skills advance.

Shooting archery won't require you to run laps or work up a sweat, but you should still dress accordingly. Put on closed-toed footwear, such as sneakers. Avoid wearing baggy clothing that could catch the bowstring if your lesson is outside and dress appropriately for the weather. If you have long hair, pull it back from your face or wear it in a ponytail. When releasing the arrow, you'll bring the bowstring back toward your face since you don't want it to tangle in your hair.

After giving archery a try, you'll become addicted and want to incorporate it into your daily life. Continue your classes and consider the kind of bow you wish to shoot while you learn about the many archery disciplines.

CHAPTER 1

COMMON TYPES OF BOWS

When you shop for a bow, you'll have a lot of fantastic options. The choice of the proper kind of bow is the challenging part. A lot relies on your preferences and demands. Some people base their bow type decision on what they think is hip. Others choose a bow based on their objectives and intended uses. Let's look at some possibilities to assist you in choosing "the one."

OLYMPIC RECURVE

The noise of the crowd dies down as your national anthem begins. The medal you wear around your neck is a symbol of years of effort and sacrifice, but it was worth it to achieve this incredible moment. An Olympic recurve might be in your future if that is your ambition. That kind of bow is preferred by thousands of leisure archers, as well as by Olympians. Olympic archery combines physical activity and mental discipline, and recurve shooting is a terrific, demanding sport.

These bows are suitable for field, indoor, and 3D archery. Adults fire targets at 70 meters in outdoor target competitions, such as the Olympics. Your Olympic bow requires different accessories than those used on other recurves in order to fire that far accurately.

A riser and two limbs make up the three primary components of an Olympic recurve. The bow can be customized and transported by disassembling it. You hold onto the riser of the bow, which is also where the arrow rest and sight are attached. When drawn, the bow's limbs bend together to provide power. Archers draw back the bowstring, causing the limbs to spring forward and launch the arrow toward the target.

The riser of an Olympic bow protrudes long rods. These stabilizers aid archers in keeping the bow steady for accurate aiming. A sight, clicker, and arrow rest are among its additional attachments. Recurve bows are less complicated than the following kind of bow.

COMPOUND BOW

Because they can shoot with amazing speed and ferocity, these bows are a favorite among bowhunters. Nevertheless, a large number of people utilize compound bows for target and competitive shooting.

There are rounded wheels that hold the draw string if you look at the top and bottom of the bow. They are known as "cams." They are a component of a levering apparatus, which also consists of cables and pulleys, that enables the bow to increase (or "compound") the force applied to propel the arrow.

Your target is 50 meters away. You set the precise distance on your sight and get ready to fire. You can see the target clearly through your magnified scope at full draw. Your release-aid "breaks" and releases the bowstring as you apply consistent pressure to it, sending your arrow flying into the 10-ring.

Consider a compound bow if you enjoy shooting accurately. These bows have a high degree of accuracy. You'll constantly strike the center with instruction. For fun, competition, or bowhunting, you can shoot compounds.

Different compound bows are used for various purposes. The sole purpose of target compound bows is precision. They offer fantastic shooting opportunities. For optimal accuracy, you can rig them up and adorn them. They have lengthy stabilizers and precisely adjustable magnifying sights as target accessories.

Hunting compounds are more compact and lighter than target bows since they need to be accurate and portable. Typically, their accessories are stronger to handle outside dangers. That doesn't mean you can't use hunting bows to compete or shoot targets. In fact, you can participate in divisions specifically for them or switch up a few accessories to take on target archers.

You have a variety of compounds to choose from if you enjoy archery for leisure. Your bow can even be made to order. You can select a compound that suits your needs if you enjoy the adaptability of a target sight and the portability of a hunting bow.

Traditional Bows

ENGLISH LONGBOW

It's likely that if you think about archery, you thought of Robin Hood. The most fundamental (and entertaining) type of archery you can use is an English longbow. A straightforward stick and string that makes use of the archers' talent and intuition. Of all the bow kinds, it is the most difficult and gratifying to use. No two bows are alike; each bow is distinctive. with feather fletchings and wooden arrows.

AMERICAN FLATBOW

Likewise called an American longbow. It was created in the 1930s. This bow design gained popularity with the aid of Howard Hill. For target shooting, the English longbow was superseded by the American flatbow. American flatbows were modernized into Olympic-style recurve bows. Flat bows are made of fiberglass and veneers of wood like red oak and black locust.

HORSE BOW

A bow design used by archers in the Eastern/Asiatic continent for ages. shorter than a longbow, some of which have hard limp points (Siyahs). Usually fired from a horse, although it can also be used without one.

RECURVE VS. LONGBOW

Uncertain of the best bow style for you? Need assistance with some wooden bow fundamentals? Your choice should be aided by this.

Longbow: Depending on how you define "Longbow". A longbow is typically used in the UK to refer to the traditional English longbow from the Middle Ages with a D-shaped design. A longbow can be an American Flatbow, also referred to as an American Longbow, in Europe and the rest of the world. Used for hunting and target shooting since the 1930s.

Recurve bows: Recurve bows are smaller than longbows in length. simpler to employ in challenging environments. These bows come in a wide range. Weights, stabilisers, clickers, lengthy rods, and sights are all features of Olympic type recurves. One-piece or takedown recurves are the norm. Change the limbs on a takedown to alter the bow's poundage.

Why shoot a longbow?

Do you wish to communicate with your ancient, battle-tested ancestors? Do you enjoy laughing a lot and having a good time? This bow will be ideal for you if the answer is yes. Victorian-style target bows and military warbows with longer draws are examples of various designs. This is why we enjoy traditional archery so much. Fire feather-fleshed wooden arrows from a longbow. Never use carbon shafts when shooting one. You'll soon realize why using this bow to shoot wooden arrows makes you so happy. An English Longbow can be picked up quickly, and knowing how to use one will be entertaining for the rest of your life.

Why would you want to shoot a recurve bow?

When learning, the majority of people will begin with a recurve bow. There is a rationale for this. Everyone, regardless of age, can easily find and use recurve bows, and they are incredibly forgiving to shoot. It's simpler to shoot recurve arrows from a shelf than from your hand. A recurve's handle resembles a pistol grip. This bow type can suit you if you want a wide variety of arrow materials. Consider a takedown recurve if transportation is a concern and you would prefer to pack the bow into a compact case.

What size longbow do I need?

As a general rule, a longbow should fit your height plus a few inches. The bow won't feel smooth to draw if you shoot one that is too short. When the draw is too lengthy, the extra height of the limbs causes energy to be wasted.

LONGBOW STRINGING TECHNIQUES

A longbow can be strung in a variety of ways. There are step-through and push-pull techniques. We advise all of our clients to string their longbows with a double loop. With this technique, the limbs are not twisted and are under an equal amount of stress. Additionally, because you have total control over the stringing procedure, it is safer. Your bow's lifespan will be increased by using a stringer, which will keep it in top condition.

How to shoot a longbow

You should be aware that we will concentrate on the right-hand shooters in this instruction before moving on to the steps.

Thus, if you are a left-handed person, you simply need to mirror the procedure. After clearing that up, let's begin the steps.

Step 1: Take a proper stance.

Getting into the proper stance is the most important stage for beginners when shooting a longbow. To begin, you must face the target at a 90-degree angle. Maintain a distance between your feet that is shoulder-width apart. You should also maintain a level head while standing straight. The body weight should be evenly distributed between the two feet. Maintain a distance between your feet that is shoulder-width apart. You should also maintain a level head while standing straight. The body weight should be evenly distributed between the two feet.

One tip for beginners would be to take an open stance by slightly rotating the left foot in the direction of the target. This will enable you to master the longbow target shooting position and succeed in the session.

Step 2: Pay Attention to Grip

Without understanding how to handle the longbow, no longbow shooting technique can be executed properly. Basically, you need to use your left hand to grasp the bow. Put your index finger and thumb between the webbing and the dish portion of the handle. Once you have the hang of the grip, shooting a standard longbow becomes more manageable. But the secret is to experiment. Start off with a softer grip. Make sure the area of your palm directly below the thumb is resting there. The fingers should then be loosely encircled by the handle. Your knuckles must remain at a 45-degree angle. And keep in mind that if you grasp the bow too tightly, it will be difficult for you to fire a longbow accurately.

Step 3: Finger and Arrow Placement

The location of the finger and arrow when using a longbow is another essential aspect. It is necessary to hold the bow about at waist level. Hold the arrow in your right hand. Eight inches should separate it from the nock end. The shaft should then be rotated so that the feather is pointed away from the riser.

The nock's throat must then be snapped onto the stringer directly below the brass string nock locator.

Next, place your right hand's three fingers on the string. The ring finger and middle finger will be directly below the nock, and the index finger will be directly above it. Keep the fingers in front of the first joint and on the string. They ought to be at a 90-degree angle to the line.

Step 4: Draw

The draw step in traditional longbow shooting determines whether or not your arrow will hit its target. This is the reason why, when learning to shoot a longbow, you must master this step. However, in order to perform the draw process, you must raise the bow vertically. Keep the bow arm's elbow rotating. When you pull the bow, it ought to be pointed directly downward. You should stand up straight, drawing arm parallel to the arrow. You should always have two drawing techniques on hand. The first technique is maintaining order as you draw back.

The second is referred to as a rotational draw. When you sketch, your back muscles are heavily used. The elbow must also be rotated while remaining at the same height. The stick with the rotational draw would be our recommendation in this scenario.

Step 5: Anchor

You need to have a clear understanding of the anchor point in order to learn how to fire a longbow automatically. In essence, it marks the end of the draw sequence as a reference point. Different anchor positions exist. However, to find out which one suits you the most, you must test them all out to see which one makes you feel more at ease.

The side anchor, however, is the most typical. It is there that your index finger should be tucked into the corner of your mouth. There is an issue with this anchor point, though. In other words, the soft tissues in the corner of your mouth can move. Therefore, stop the drawing cycle on a hard bone rather than the mouth. One such tooth is the one that lies immediately below your eye.

Step 6: Release

You must concentrate on the area you wish to shoot the arrow at after you have arrived at the anchor point. You'll have to use your sighting technique in this situation. And regardless of the sighting technique you use, you shouldn't keep your attention on the target for more than a few seconds. Your aim will be off if you don't. All that's left to do is release the arrow once you've achieved the proper aim. You just have to relax your fingers and release the string during the release process.

Finally, be careful not to move abnormally following the release. If that's the case, you won't be able to act after the shot.

RECURVE BOW SHOOTING TECHNIQUES

The following procedures should be used when shooting a recurve bow:

Step 1

Place your feet shoulder-width apart and perpendicular to the target while standing straight.

Make sure your dominant hand is farthest (behind) the target. The "square stance" refers to this.

Stand with your feet shoulder-width apart, and in this case, right (dominant) hand "behind" the target

Step 2

Nock the arrow by positioning the arrow shaft down on your bow's rest or arrow shelf. Connect the bowstring to the nock, or notch, on the back of the arrow. Some store-bought bows may even have a nock locator or two to indicate where the nock goes; if there are two locators, position the nock between them. Nock the arrow underneath the sole locator if there are any. If your bow doesn't have locators, nock the arrow parallel to and in the middle of the bowstring. If your bow is a homemade creation and lacks nock locators and a nock shelf, nock the arrow in the middle of the bow and bowstring. Some store-bought bows at least contain an arrow shelf as a reference. A simple notch, hook, or even a part of the bow, like in the example above, can serve as an arrow shelf on some bows. In order to reduce friction and prevent a drop in acceleration when the arrow is released, some arrow shelves may even feature a tuft of fur.

Step 3

Hold the bow in your non-dominant hand. Be sure to hold the bow with the pad of your thumb resting on the arrow rest, or just below the place where you nock the arrow. If your knuckles are at a 45-degree angle with the bow's grip region, you are holding the bow correctly. The bow will then rest properly on your thumb's pad. Avoid holding the bow too firmly as this can cause the bow to torque inward, which will lead you to miss your target. To get the perfect grip, create an imaginary handshake with the bow while maintaining a neutral grip.

With your "weak" hand, hold the bow while making sure your knuckles are at a 45-degree angle.

Step 4

Use your index, middle, and ring fingers to hold the bowstring. The nock of the bow should be situated between your index and middle fingers, with the bowstring resting in the crook formed by your upper knuckles. Wear a glove or a finger tab if you find the bowstring to be painful or uncomfortable. With your index, middle, and ring fingers, grab the bowstring.

Make sure the arrow is nocked between your middle and index fingers.

If holding an arrow causes you too much discomfort or anguish, invest in or manufacture your own archery finger tab.

Step 5

Maintain your steady bow-handling arm at roughly shoulder height. Draw back the bowstring with your fingers while maintaining a tight grip. Most archery beginners draw the bowstring back with their arm, bicep, and shoulder, but doing so can make you more exhausted and won't allow you to pull the bowstring back far enough to provide the most power.

Consider pushing your shoulder blades together while you make an effort to "activate" your back muscles. Draw the bowstring back with your shoulder and arm, but not entirely.

Pull the bowstring back by using your back muscles. New archers frequently make the error of relying solely on their shoulder and arm muscles.

Step 6

Pick your anchor point, which can be a spot on your nose or the corner of your mouth. This is where you draw the bowstring closest to you. Use this consistently both when you are practicing and actually shooting at a target, no matter which component you choose to serve as your anchor point.

It's crucial to keep the bow steady when you match the arrow's tip with your target. As you practice your technique, don't worry about external elements like the wind direction. Keep your attention on the goal.

Concentrate primarily on getting the arrow to meet the target while you practice your aim.

Avoid "overthinking" this procedure.

Step 7

Simply push your fingers on the bowstring out of the way to release the arrow while maintaining your bow steady and pointed at your target. Allow your hand to move backwards until it reaches a place below your ears after releasing the bowstring.

Don't interfere with the bow's forward motion; doing so will allow it to advance a little and give the arrow additional energy. In order to give the arrow more energy to fly farther and strike the target with greater force, it is important to keep your dominant hand moving after you release the arrow. Bring your hand back to behind your head and allow the bow to tilt forward slightly.

Recurve or longbow: which is superior?

You want the truth, right? That all depends on you, your archery technique, your form, and the results you hope to achieve with a bow. It is not true that one bow is superior to another. It all comes down to how the bow feels and how you connect with the shot when using traditional archery. We often say that the customer is chosen by the bow. Due to our extensive experience working with archers, we are aware that what may be effective for one archer may not be effective for another. You can see what we mean by shooting two identical bows at the store.

CHAPTER 2

ARCHERY KIT

Although you can get as technical with archery as you like, most people will start with some basic tools. As you advance, you might discover that customizing your equipment can help you shoot better and use better technique.

Supplies one will need to start archery

A bow, a string, some arrows, a bracer, finger tab, a quiver, a bow stand, a bow stringer, and a target to shoot at are all you really need if you want to join a club and shoot frequently after your beginner's course. All other equipment will be provided.

You'll need some basic equipment for your bow and arrows to finish your archery setup.

QUIVER

Your arrows are held in a quiver when you shoot. You can embrace your inner Robin Hood by selecting a back quiver. You can also choose a waist quiver for your belt or a bow quiver that attaches to your bow.

RELEASE AND FINGER TAB

Finger tabs and release-aids keep your fingers safe while assisting with a clean bowstring release. A trigger mechanism is used by mechanical releasing aids. The jaws or a clip on the release secure it to the bowstring. A D-loop, which is a brief piece of cord tied into a loop right below where the arrow's nock grips the string, is present on the bowstring of the majority of compound bows. The D-loop is attached by the release-aid. The archer draws the bow, takes aim, and squeezes the release-trigger aid's with the thumb or index finger after attaching the release to the D-loop. The release-aid releases the string to fire the arrow when the trigger is squeezed. The trigger mechanism of the release-aid contributes to its astounding precision. There are two fundamental types of mechanical releases: wrist-strap and handheld. Your wrist is connected to wrist-strap releases via a clasp or Velcro strap. Due of its low cost and ease of use, that style is preferred by the majority of beginner compound archers. Archers hold the bowstring at the first joint of their fingers and release it using their index, middle, and ring fingers. Then they draw the bow, take their aim, and let go of the bowstring by relaxing their fingers. When shooting their bows, recurve and longbow archers cover their fingers with a glove or finger tab. Leather finger tabs and gloves are available in a variety of sizes. Your fingers and the bowstring are separated by a finger tab. The tab shouldn't dangle over your fingertips, but it should still cover your three fingers. Use scissors to cut the tab for a precise fit. Similar to a leather work glove, a shooting glove merely protects the tips of your shooting fingers. The glove fastens around your wrist and has leather fingertip parts. You can try on different sizes of shooting gloves in the pro shop.

ARM GUARD

A bowstring goes by your forearm as you release it. It can hurt if the bowstring scrapes against your forearm. An armguard shields your forearm from the bowstring and stops the string from catching on your shirt or coat sleeves as it passes.

BOW CASE

Put your bow and accessories in a soft case or hard case. When you travel between your house and the range, your bow is protected with a bow case. Unprotected bows can sustain damage if they are dropped on concrete or struck by a car, door, or wall. The most protective casings are the hard ones. The majority are approved for air travel, so you can bring your bow on vacation or to far-off events. Some types can be secured for security and incorporate wheels for simple rolling and movement. However, soft cases are adequate for the majority of archers. They keep your kit organized, shield your bow from nicks and dings, and are lighter than hard cases. Some soft cases are better suited for road excursions, while others are approved for air travel.

ACCESSORIES AND OTHER TOOLS

A bow stand to hold your bow when you're not shooting; arrow lube and an arrow puller to make it easy to remove arrows from targets; string wax to protect your bowstring and keep it looking new. Additional equipment you might need includes: a bow-stringer for stringing your recurve or longbow; Allen wrenches for adjusting your sights or maintaining your bow; a bow stand to hold your bow when you're not shooting.

Target

A target is made up of three components: a boss that safely stops the arrows, typically made of tightly packed rubber or straw; a target face that is typically made of reinforced paper; and a stand that secures the boss and target face.

You'll have everything you need to enjoy archery at home or on the range with these necessities.

Before you purchase your own, your club may have equipment you can use.

THE BASICS PARTS OF A BOW:

Here are some terms you might hear when talking about bows before we move on. Recurve and compound bows are both covered in the sections below:

The Riser

The riser is the gripping portion of the bow, located in its center. The same applies to compound, recurve, and barebow weapons. They can be either left- or right-handed depending on the person. When you shoot, you hold the bow's handle in your hand. The arrow rest, which is where you place your arrows before drawing, is a feature of the riser. Risers are complicated, but here's what you need to know right now. Compound bows typically have a containment rest, while recurve bows typically have an elevated rest, which is essentially just a platform that the arrow sits on. Known as a "whisker biscuit," this type of containment rest is one of the most common.

The Limbs

These are fastened to the riser and make up the actual bow, with the top limb being connected to the bottom limb by the bow string. When referring to recurve bows, the term "takedown bow" is frequently used; this refers to a bow whose old limbs can be removed and swapped out for newer, heavier ones. Takedown bows are excellent for new users since you may add more limbs as your strength and accuracy increase.

Bowstring

The string that connects the top limb of the bow to the bottom limb of the bow is the one that shoots your arrows.

The Nock Point

The end of the arrow should be placed here on the bow string. To reliably aim and fire, the nocking point must remain in the same location.

Bow Sight

When properly adjusted, the bow sight works a lot like the scope on a rifle; it enables you to aim at your target. Although many bows include sights, many archers choose to enhance. Sights are often mounted to the riser and are easily removable as needed.

Pressure button

The pressure button on the bows of barebow and recurve archers is used to assist in fine-tuning the arrows. This promotes accuracy. A pressure button helps the arrows leave the bow smoothly when they are shot since arrows bend when they are fired.

Clicker

A recurve bow uses a clicker to make sure the string is always drawn back to the same spot before the arrow is released. The clicker is positioned beneath the arrow, and when it is drawn back, it will sound to signal the archer to release the bow.

Arrow rest

An arrow rest is a simple device that attaches to the riser of the bow and supports the arrow throughout the shooting process. It is made to hold the arrow in the proper place and is flexible enough to not get in the way as the arrow takes off. For both left- and right-handed bows, there are arrow rests available.

Arrows

Arrows can be made of wood, aluminum, carbon, or a mixture of carbon and aluminum. It's crucial to select the ideal arrow stiffness and length for you. Never use an arrow that is too short since it could slip off the arrow rest as you draw it, harm the bow, or even worse, harm you. Before purchasing new arrows, verify with your club first as some archery organizations have restrictions on the types of arrows you are permitted to use.

Shaft

The shaft is the primary body of the arrow and is typically made of carbon or aluminum tubes or solid wood.

Nock

An arrow's nock is the groove where it attaches to the bow string at the end of the arrow.

Fletchings

These feather or plastic attachments are fastened to the back of the arrow shaft and aid in stabilizing the arrow while it is in flight.

The arrow's tip serves as the pile. To assist the arrow fly straight, they are frequently pile fashioned of a heavier metal than the shaft.

Don't worry if it all looks like too much information. In little time at all, you will comprehend the specifics of those terms.

5 MAIN TYPES OF ARCHERY

Target archery, field archery, hunting, traditional archery, and three-dimensional archery are the five main categories of archery. Which of these styles you plan to shoot will determine the type of bow you need. This two archery disciplines do occasionally overlap; for example, many archers who shoot target archery also shoot field archery. It is therefore best to purchase a bow that not only primarily complements your primary archery style but also functions at least passably in any other archery you may be interested in.

Targets are shot at in both indoor and outdoor target archery. You have probably seen targets of this type a million times over the years. They are the standard circle within a circle targets. In target archery, competitors aim straight at the targets, shoot, and then receive a judge's score.

In that archers shoot at (three or four different types of) targets, field archery is similar to target archery. In contrast to target archery, where the targets are always in a straight line, field archery targets can be up a hill above you or down in a valley.

Tree branches, brush, or another type of obstruction could also be partially obstructing your view of the target. Small groups of archers often shoot while following a course or path through the woods and pausing to aim at each target.

Hunting shouldn't require much explanation because it is simple enough. When hunting animals that they are permitted to do so by their state or local jurisdiction, hunters merely use bows.

Traditional archery does not follow the same standards as target or field archery in terms of guidelines, rules, and regulations. Like archers have done for thousands of years prior, traditional archers use longbows or solid-body, wooden recurve bows. Traditional archery is less of a competition and more about returning to old shooting techniques. Traditional shooting does not use stabilizers, fancy bow sights, or any other contemporary technology.

Field archery and 3D archery share certain similarities in that both sports involve walking a course through the woods. The difference is that you are firing at life-size 3D animal replicas instead.

A small group of you will move along the path while stopping at each target to fire. Additionally, there are 3D shooting competitions and shootings with rewards for the best shooters.

OTHER TYPES OF ARCHERY

• Clout Archery: Shooting at a flag from a predetermined distance, which varies by age and gender and can be up to 180 yards away. Score areas surrounding the flag on the ground

• Flight Archery: Launching an arrow as far as possible. the chosen bow type's best distance is scored.

As I previously stated, the kind of bow you should purchase will be largely based on which of these shooting techniques you intend to use. Now, let's quickly go over them:

Modern Recurve Bows

Modern recurve bows are defined as having multiple detachable parts and/or being made of more than one material. Modern bows, in contrast to one-piece wooden recurve bows, may have fiberglass or carbon limbs, while the riser (the central portion of the bow that you hold with your bow hand) may be made of wood. A lot of modern recurves are also take-down bows, which means that the limbs can be separated, making them much simpler to store. Additionally, since you may alter the limbs, you can also alter the draw weight of the bow you're using.

Consider a scenario in which you want to upgrade from shooting a thirty-pound bow to one that weighs forty-five pounds. Purchasing new bow limbs is much less expensive than purchasing an entirely new bow.

Their Functions Are:

Modern recurves are arguably the most adaptable kind of bow because they work well for almost all archery disciplines. Target, field, and 3D archery all use them.

Recurve bows can be used for hunting as well, but you must make sure that the draw weight is at least forty or fifty pounds.

Compound Bows

Compound bows were created with hunting in mind. Their main advantage is that you only need to hold back a small portion of the bow's total draw weight after fully drawing it back.

Unlike other bows, the cam and pulley system at each end of the bow supports the majority of the draw weight. This makes it easier for an archer to hold the bow back for longer periods of time.

Target archery and field archery both use compound bows, though not as frequently as recurve bows, the only kind permitted in Olympic target archery.

Compound bows are primarily used for hunting, though they can also be used for other forms of archery.

Longbows and Wooden Recurve Bows

For traditional archery, the preferred bows are longbows and one-piece hardwood recurve bows. They can also be utilized in 3D, field, and target archery.

The best sorts of bows for you would be a longbow or a wooden recurve if your primary interest is traditional archery. You may still shoot them in various sorts of archery, but they're not as as advanced as many of the more modern bows.

They are excellent for traditional archery but can also be used in various forms of the sport.

Once you've determined out what forms of archery you're interested in as well as the type of bow you'll require, you'll need to select the correct arrows for your bow.

Today arrows are created from many various sorts of materials, each one having their own strengths and disadvantages. These days, arrows are fashioned from various materials, including fiberglass, carbon, aluminum, an aluminum-carbon hybrid, and wood.

CHAPTER 3

EYE DOMINANCE

You must first choose which eye is your "dominant eye" before going over the steps for launching a bow. The majority of the time, but not always, your "dominant eye" will be the same as your "dominant hand." Being "cross-dominant" refers to someone having a dominant eye that is opposite their dominant hand.

Perform the "wink test" as described below to find out if your left or right eye is dominant:

1. As if requesting someone to halt, place your hands in front of you with the palms facing outward.

2. Align your thumbs so that the tips of both of them touch.

3. Make a triangle between your hands by turning your hands inward so that the tips of your index fingers contact.

4. Continue to squeeze your hands together until a smaller but passable triangle is formed.

5. Make use of the triangle to "point" at an object that is a few meters away from you; it must fit inside the triangle.

6. Switch back and forth between "winking" your left and right eyes. You'll notice that one eye won't be able to see the object in the triangle, but the other will. Your dominant eye is the one that allows you to see the object.

PROPER SHOOTING FORM

Nearly all archers will concur that form and accuracy are the two aspects of archery that are most crucial. In any form of archery, proper form is essential. It's crucial to focus on having good form right away since it's far simpler to acquire a good habit than it is to replace a bad one.

Make sure you don't begin archery with a bow that has a draw weight that is too hefty for you if you're a beginner. Starting small and moving up the ladder is a far better strategy. Because recurve bow limbs are lighter and improper form could cause the bow to twist, which would cause arrows to deviate off course, form is especially crucial for recurve bow archers.

Your Shot Sequence

An alternative term for "everything you do when you shoot each arrow" is a shot sequence. So, for instance, the shot sequence would be: Standing up straight, nocking your arrow, drawing your bow back, pointing, and then releasing the arrow. The basic shot sequence that follows will get you started shooting right away. As you get more experience, you can always modify it up.

Correct Posture

If you are a right-handed person, hold your bow in your left hand while standing at a 90-degree angle to the target. indicating that the outside of your left foot should be pointed directly at the target. As you draw the bow back, keep your posture in mind as you stand with your feet shoulder-width apart. From the time the bow is drawn back until the arrow strikes the target, your eyes should be open and fixed on it.

Nocking the Arrow

Simply put, the nock is the portion of the arrow's back that hooks onto the bow string. Under the nocking point, cock the arrow (the metal ring on the bowstring). Make sure the arrow nocks onto the bow string with an audible click. For the majority of setups, the index feather the unusually colored feather or vane on your arrow should be facing away from the bow. For compound bows with drop-away arrow rests or other configurations, this may differ.

Bowstring Grip

When you pull back the bow and release the arrow, there are a number different methods to hold the bowstring; we'll go over a few of them here. To begin with, you shouldn't even be holding the arrow. If the arrow is correctly nocked, the nock ought to be able to cling onto the bowstring on its own. Only the actual bowstring should be held in your fingers' grip.

Utilize your index, middle, and ring fingers to hold the bow string. Use only the meaty portion of your fingers, extending past the tips but not all the way to the first joint.

Either place all three fingers underneath the arrow or place the index finger above it and the other two fingers below it. While the second is referred to as shooting "three under," the first is known as shooting "split finger."

Use whichever feels more natural and at ease for you among these. If you don't want to hold the bow with your fingers, you might also use a release assistance. A release aid is only a tiny device that grips the bowstring and pulls a trigger to release it.

Drawing the Bow

Draw back the string along your bow arm (or your left arm if you're right handed) to draw the bow. To return to the anchor point on your face, pull the bow in a straight line. When you are shooting at the target, your anchor point is where you are holding your draw hand at full draw.

For most people, this is typically the chin, nose, or upper cheek. Try to focus on using your back muscles as you draw the bow back. Your shoulder blades ought to incline toward one another.

Anchor Point

Use the anchor point that, in your opinion, feels the most secure and natural. It will be easier to aim with your sight if the bow string touches both your chin and your nose while using a bow sight. The index finger is positioned at this anchor point directly below your mandible. You should close your mouth and clench your teeth. You shouldn't have anything obstructing you, therefore refrain from chewing gum.

When you have the bow back at full draw, your bow hand, elbow, and draw hand should all be in a straight line. keeping your shoulders even with this line, but still maintaining a comfortable stance.

Take Aim

Aim at the target. If you choose to fire your bow without a sight, you can utilize a bow sight or other aiming methods.

Release the Arrow

Continue to bring your shoulder blades together as you release the arrow, keeping your draw hand's fingers loose enough that, as you reach the proper point, the arrow nearly releases by itself.

Follow Through

With every shot, it's crucial to follow through effectively. To see how well you shot, don't rush to drop your bow. Wait until you hear each arrow hit its target after you unleash it before moving. If you're holding the bow correctly, it will drop naturally into your bow hand.

If you're having trouble with this, make it a habit to count to five after each arrow is fired before you move.

So there you have it; you are now prepared to go outside and practice shooting. We've pretty much covered all the essentials; if there are any additional topics you need to learn, check out other chapters and subtopics on this guide. Get outside right away and enjoy yourself.

ARCHERY LESSONS AND PROGRAMS FOR NEW ARCHERS

Try out the sport at an archery store as your first step in learning to use a bow and arrow. Once you've mastered the fundamentals of archery, you might want to enroll in a course or more experienced lessons.

Group/private lessons

Because you have the instructor's full attention for 30 minutes, one-on-one lessons speed up learning. Consider making your lessons an hour long as you get better. Group lessons are an additional choice and an enjoyable, social method to study. Many businesses provide both adult and child group lessons. To find out your alternatives, get in touch with a bow shop. Whether through schools, pro shops, community centers, or archery/bowhunting clubs, programs offer more avenues to learn archery.

Junior olympic archery development

A wonderful method to expose yourself to high level competition is to start in the JOAD program.

For children aged 8 to 20, USA Archery offers the JOAD program. Usually, these weekly group courses take place at stores, clubs, or shooting ranges. They assist archers in honing their abilities in a group setting at their own speed. Participants in group archery sessions get to know other archers while getting individualized instruction from qualified teachers. Similar to other organized sports, parents play a significant role in JOAD sessions. The Adult Archery program from USA Archery provides the same advantages as JOAD, such as chances to get physical activity, make new friends, and boost self-confidence. It serves archers who are 21 and older.

Olympic archery in the schools

OAS is an entertaining youth program that presents kids with both mental and physical difficulties. OAS instructs Olympic-style archery, as the name suggests. Participants in a national mail-in tournament participate both individually and in teams.

National archery in the schools program

Another excellent opportunity for students to participate in archery is through NASP. NASP is a classroom exercise that introduces students to the fundamentals of archery using Genesis bows and arrows that are suitable for users of all ages. NASP archers aim an 80-centimeter target from a distance of 5 to 15 yards. NASP also finances contests in which schools participate from all around the country, including locally.

Scholastic 3d archery

A great next step program for pupils to shoot 3D targets after school is Scholastic 3D Archery. Both indoors and outside, these life-size, three-dimensional animal targets are fired. All equipment is permitted, including simple bows, Olympic recurves, and compound bows. The program provides after-school lessons in addition to regional and international competitions. These enjoyable competitions are great for enhancing college résumés.

Explore archery

A program called Explore Archery introduces newbies to the activity. It can be taken as a one-day, one-week, six-week, or one-off event class. Students learn everything in the program, from easy games and enjoyable competitions to basic archery form.

Archers USA

With an unsighted bow and few accuracy-improving accoutrements, many beginners begin archery. For camps and other programs where numerous people must shoot the same bow, simple bows are ideal. In certain circumstances, shooting a naked bow makes sense because sights, release aids, and peep sights need to be individually calibrated for each archer, which requires time and consideration. A sight, release, peep-sight, and draw-weight adjustment system was created by Archers USA to make it simple and quick for archers to set up. The system's numbered adjustments also make it simple for retailers or teachers to adapt the bow to each archer's preferences. After receiving an Archers USA bow, archers are given a code that instructs a professional how to adjust the bow to their specifications. Tools are not necessary for these changes. These distinctive bows are brought into schools by the "varsity" program for shooting during or after the school day.

To find out which group or private sessions are offered, speak to your archery instructor or get in touch with the program managers.

FUN WAYS TO ENJOY YOUR BOW

Archers can have fun with their bows in many different ways, from playing games in the backyard to competing on a global scale. Let's look at some possibilities.

Shoot balloons

It's a lot more fun to shoot balloons and play archery games than to play bocce ball or corn hole. When you strike your mark, enjoy the delightful "pop" by securing the balloons to the target and shooting.

For extra more excitement, you may also fill balloons with paint, cornstarch, or glitter. Don't use hardware store paint. Homemade paint that is easier to clean up and more environmentally friendly can be made.

Recipe for Homemade Paint

- 1/2 cup flour; 1/2 cup salt; 1/2 cup water; 1/4 teaspoon food coloring

Salt, water, and flour should be thoroughly combined. Add food coloring until the desired shade is achieved.

Stump shooting

Roving, also known as stump-shooting, is one of the earliest archery sports. Simply locate a dead tree stump, choose a location there, and fire. Throwing arrows and making ordinary walks in the woods into adventures will make you feel like a child. Stump-shooting is legal on private property with permission, on public lands, and at home. To find out if it's legal in your area, contact the wildlife department of your state. Use a judo, which is an arrow point, while firing at stumps. Wire claws are also on these blunt points. The claws stop arrows from digging into grass, and the blunt point inhibits penetration into stumps.

Null stumps? No issue. Archery shops sell targets in the form of balls. Pull your arrows, throw the circular target, fire it where it stops, and then repeat.

FIELD, 3D AND TARGET ARCHERY

All summer long, field, 3D, and target archery are enjoyable. Try field or 3D archery if you enjoy trekking. Target archery is your sport if you enjoy shooting on a grassy area. For events, inquire with your local archery club or visit larger competitions held elsewhere in the nation. These shooting sports are available for recreation and competition.

You may watch field, 3D, and target events online if it's raining. Watch the top archers in the world compete. Learn the various disciplines of archery and observe their form. It's an excellent method to learn the game and develop a devoted following.

Which Kind of Bow Should You Start Out With?

We'll break up our responses to this excellent question into two parts:

When choosing your first bow for yourself as an adult, there is no correct response, but the following are the key considerations:

Recurve bows are typically simpler to use and purchase. Just make sure your dimensions are accurate (and we help you with that below). They require less fine-tuning, and many versions may be assembled "straight out of the box" and used for shooting. For a beginner archer, simplicity like that makes it easy to get started in the sport.

Compound bows might be a little more challenging to tune because of their cams and accessories, so if you purchase one online, you might need to take it to a local shop or archery facility to have it tuned (some models have videos on YouTube that show you what you need to do, though, and that can make things a lot easier). Compound bows have the advantage of being much simpler to aim and shoot once they are properly tuned, which makes hitting your target much simpler. Most archers find great satisfaction in consistently hitting their target. However, as we have stated, the decision is ultimately up to you. Use compound bows if you're inclined to them; start with recurve bows if you prefer their aesthetic. There is no correct response; your decision is entirely your own. Many archers employ both during the course of their careers. Those interested in target archery typically use recurve bows, which are made to improve form and accuracy, while those interested in bowhunting typically use compound bows, which are made to be compact and transportable through hunting environments and shoot arrows that are blisteringly fast and powerful. But those are just generalizations, as I indicated. There are many target archers who compete in events where competitors use compound bows, and many hunters who put in a lot of practice and utilize recurve bows designed for hunting.

OUR BOW RECOMMENDATIONS FOR NEW ARCHERS

Over the years, we've examined a lot of bows, and there are two that we believe are the best choices for beginning archers.

ADULT RECOMMENDATIONS

Samick Sage Archery 62-inch Takedown Recurve Bow, 25–60 lb., Right & Left Handed

• SIZE: The Samick Sage Recurve bow has a 62-inch length, a 28-inch draw length, and a draw weight range of 25 to 60 pounds.

Riser, 2 fiberglass laminated limbs, 14 strands of dacron bowstring, a stick-on arrow rest, and installation instructions are all included. The individual limbs are replaceable and available for purchase.

• Right-handed people should hold the bow in their LEFT hand and pull the string with their RIGHT hand. Left-handed: Use your RIGHT hand to hold the bow and your LEFT hand to pull the string.

We virtually always recommend the Samick Sage Recurve Bow for recurves. Our favorite, It's simple to use, simple to put up, and simple to accessorize you can easily add an arrow rest and a bow sight. Additionally, because it is a "take-down" bow, you may swap out the limbs if you wish to make the bow stronger or weaker. Many archers have utilized it to go from the "beginning" stage to the "intermediate" stage since it is strong and dependable. It's a fantastic choice for both young people and adults.

Adult Compound Bow with Left and Right Hands, Hunting Kit with 5 Pin Lighted Sight, Quiver, String Stop, Stabilizer, Shock Absorber, and Allen Tool Pull force and cams Target sheets that are totally adjustable.

• PERFECT PLATFORM - This fantastic, one-of-a-kind bow offers versatility and strength for adults, youth, beginning, and intermediate archers, as well as right- and left-handed compound bows!

• COMPLETELY ADJUSTABLE - With an axle length of 30" and a weight of just 3.6 lbs, the draw length can be altered from 24.5" to 31", and the draw weight may be changed from 30 lbs to 70 lbs without the need for an archery compound bow press, as big bows typically do!

• HIGH QUALITY MACHINING - All aluminum components, including the cams and modules, were used in the manufacturing process. Compound design has a split yoke tuning mechanism that allows for fine adjustments for appropriate arrow flight and provides for a 75% let-off.

We prefer the Predator Raptor Compound Bow for compound bows. It has an adjustable draw weight, which allows you to start out with a lower draw weight (on the Raptor, that's 30 pounds) and raise it as you develop strength and ability. If you're not sure what draw weight is, keep reading to find out. Below, we describe it. It's made with some excellent equipment, like a stabilizer to keep the bow steady, a whisker biscuit rest, and a five-pin bow sight, all of which you'll need to get started. We believe that because of its adaptability, it's a fantastic choice for people who are just getting into archery.

RECOMMENDATIONS FOR YOUNG ADULTS AND KIDS

Easton Youth Beginner Recurve Bow Kit

We typically advise the Easton Youth Beginner Recurve Kit for younger children. The bow string is simple to draw back, it has a "ambidextrous" design that makes it suitable for both right-handed and left-handed people, and it comes with some accessories, including three arrows, a hip quiver to store them in, an arm guard (essential for shooters of all ages), and a finger tab. We suggest the Samick Sage for young adults looking for recurve bows. It's a great bow that your teen or young adult can use as they mature.

Genesis Original Bow Archery Kit, Right Hand, Black

• UNIVERSAL DRAW LENGTH: A versatile compound bow design with an adjustable draw weight range of 10 to 20 pounds and a draw length range of 15 to 30 inches.

• BUILT FOR ALL AGES: This is the first compound bow created to fit everyone, with a universal draw length and adjustable weight, making it a great starter bow for all ages, athletic abilities, and the official bow of the National Archery in the Schools Program NASP).

• SIMPLE TO USE: The single cam design eliminates the need for tuning, reduces recoil, increases accuracy, and reduces noise so you can experience the pure joy of archery.

We love the Genesis Original Kit for compounds. It's a good option for beginning archers of all ages, has a draw weight range that can be adjusted from 10 to 20, and is very simple to use. That's advantageous because compound bows can become quite complex. A quiver, an arm guard, five aluminum arrows, and a hex wrench that you can use to change the draw weight of the bow are also included in the package.

Bear Archery Brave Bow Set

• An entry-level bow measuring 26" axle to axle includes two Safetyglass arrows that are ready to shoot.

• The set also contains an arrow quiver, finger rollers, an armguard, and Whisker Biscuit.

• Whisker Biscuit, a $40 value, is the safest rest in the archery industry.

After discussing some excellent possibilities, we've reached the challenging part: your measurements. You must understand how to select a bow with the proper settings if you want to find one that you can shoot safely. This can be a bit of a challenge for beginning archers, so if the sections that follow seem unclear at first, don't worry. Most beginning archers experience some confusion when taking their measurements.

HOW TO MEASURE FOR THE RIGHT-SIZED BOW FOR YOU

Draw length and draw weight are the two key dimensions you'll need to consider when choosing your first bow. Let's go over each one.

Drawing Length

Draw length, the first measurement, refers to how far you can comfortably draw back the bow string. Draw length is essential for accurate shooting because you must always pull the bow string back the same amount for each shot. Generally speaking, taller people have longer draws, and shorter people typically have shorter draws.

Your draw length can be determined in one of two ways:

1) Visit an archery shop and request a bow measurement from a bow tech using a device called a "draw length indicator shaft." The tool, which resembles a very long arrow but is actually marked with measurements, will allow the bow technician to ascertain your draw length.

2) Divide your height, measured in inches, by 2.5. As an example, if you are six feet tall, you are 72 inches tall (6 feet x 12 inches = 72 inches), and 72 divided by 2.5 becomes 28.8. So if you're six feet tall, you'd select a bow with a draw length of 29 inches (draw length in measured in full inches, so you'd round up from 28.8 to 29). Taking your height in inches and dividing by 2.5 is remarkably accurate, and seems to work for most people.

Draw Weight

The second measurement to take into account when purchasing a bow is this one. The draw weight is a unit of weight that expresses how challenging it is to draw the drawstring back. It will be very simple to draw and shoot a bow that weighs 10 pounds, while it will be more challenging to draw and shoot a bow that weighs 50 pounds or more.

Young adults between the ages of 18 and 21 do well with a draw weight between 15 and 30 pounds (again, stronger 18 to 21 year olds may be able to draw more than that), and adults 22 and older typically use bows with draw weights of 25 pounds and higher. As a general rule, children up to the age of 18 are good with bows that have a draw weight from 5 to 20 pounds (and 18 year olds may be able to draw more than that). However, these figures are only approximations, and as you get more expertise, you'll discover more about your draw weight capacity.

Recurve bows may have a "set" draw weight, which means that if you purchase one with a 25-pound draw weight, it will always have that draw weight. This is typically true with recurve bows, as the limbs are affixed to the riser permanently. However, some recurves feature limbs that you can swap out for lighter or heavier limbs to change the draw weight of the bow. These limbs are referred to as "takedown limbs" (for more information, see our "Parts of a Bow" section). A bow with takedown limbs is a great choice if you're a beginning archer because with time and practice, your strength will grow and you can use takedown limbs to increase the power of your bow.

Contrarily, compound bows are frequently adjustable by design, so you don't need to purchase additional limbs to change their weight. For many archers, that represents a significant advantage because it allows them to purchase just one bow and adjust the draw weight as necessary. Before we end, there is one more thing to think about when purchasing a bow: which hand you will use to hold the bow. The majority of the time, right-handed people will use a right-handed bow (which they hold in their left hand and draw with their right hand), and left-handed people will use a left-handed bow) (and a left-handed bow is one that you hold in your right hand, and use your left hand to draw the bow string).

BOW PACKAGES AND ADDITIONAL EQUIPMENT

While you now have a good understanding of bows, there are a few other things you might need before you start archery. Here are some extra tools you might want to research.

Arm guards

Arm guards will be our first piece of equipment because they are the most crucial. Wearing this piece of safety equipment prevents your inner arm from being hit by the bow string after you release an arrow, making it suitable for both recurve and compound bows. Although being struck by a bow string may not seem serious, it can be excruciatingly painful and leave you with a massive, three-dimensional bruise. There are many excellent arm guards available; we prefer the SAS Arm Guard because it is substantial and offers a lot of coverage. We also recommend the OMP Mountain Man Arm Guard because it has straps and Velcro and may be a little bit easier to adjust but includes buckles, which some people dislike.

SAS 8" Armguard Archery Bow Range with 3-Strap Buckles

• 8" Arm Guard with 3 Straps

- Vented to Ensure Adequate Airflow to Cool Your Arm

- Long-Lasting Archery Arm Protection

OMP Mountain Man 2-Strap Ventilated Leather Suede Arm Guard

- The arm guard is made of suede and has a two-strap Velcro construction for a snug but comfortable fit.

- Vented to ensure adequate airflow

- Arm guard is 7 Inch in length

BOW RELEASES AND/OR TABS

When you pull back the drawstring to shoot an arrow, these tools let you grab hold of it. You can do this with your fingers, but doing so will hurt a lot and cause you to miss a lot of shots.

Recurve bow releases are quite straightforward, but most shooters opt to use a glove (we recommend the Archery Max Leather Glove since it's incredibly comfortable and remains in place) or a tab (and we like the CyberDyer Leather Tab). Compound bow releases can be somewhat difficult, but for beginners, we typically suggest the TruFire Edge Foldback Release. It has a trigger release that feels quite natural, a dual caliper that improves accuracy, and you attach it to your wrist, making it simpler for novices.

ArcheryMax Handmade Leather Three Finger Archery Gloves, Black ,Small

• Materials: mesh and cow leather

Note: ArcheryMax is a brand.

• Excellent sensitivity for optimal string feel

CyberDyer Cow Leather Archery Finger Tab for Recurve Bows Hunting Finger Protector Brown

• Made of premium Cowskin material; most right-handed archers may utilize it.

• Dimensions (L x W): 7.7 cm × 6.6 cm / 3.03 in x 2.59 in ; weight: 0.52 oz / 18g.

- It might keep your fingers and arm from getting harmed while you shoot.

TruFire Edge Buckle Foldback Adjustable Archery Compound Bow Release - Wrist Strap with Foldback Design - Black or Camo

Bow Sights.

These assist you in aiming, as we indicated previously. Recurve bows frequently lack a bow sight, so we like the Recurve Bow Sight since it's simple to set up, simple to operate, and adjustable after each shot. The Archery Essentials Bow Sight is a good option if your selected compound bow does not already have one since compound bows frequently do. Compound bow sights can be extremely complex, but this model is simple to use and simple to modify.

I-Sport Archery Recurve Bow Sight Metal Target Accessory Bowsight Black 1 Set

- Lightweight, robust design; made of machined aluminum

- With thumb screws, universal mounting is simple to set up and adjust.

- Comes with bracket and attaching screws

TOPOINT ARCHERY 3 Pin Bow Sight - Fiber, Brass Pin, Aluminum Machined - Right and Left Handed

- Material:6061-T6 aluminum

- Fiber optic color: red, green, diameter: 0.029"

- Two vertical bars, level

Quivers

Hip quivers are the most popular for target shooting, and we favor the Easton Flipside Hip Quiver. However, there are several more types of quivers available, including back quivers and quivers you can attach directly to your riser. Twelve arrows fit comfortably inside, and it has several compartments for tools or other items. It clips to your belt or pants. NOTE: When purchasing a compound, be sure to confirm whether a quiver is included in the package. Quivers are a typical add-on when purchasing a compound bow and frequently attach to the riser when used for bowhunting.

Easton Flipside 3-Tube Hip Quiver

• An ambidextrous, reversible hook and loop pocket

• Bow square slot, belt clip attachment, and integrated accessory attachment grommet

• Color is Black

And lastly, arrows are possibly the most crucial piece of equipment. This will have its own section.

Without an arrow, a bow isn't a bow.

We have now discussed bows. Why not use arrows?

There are three basic categories of arrows: carbon, wood, and aluminum. Each has distinctive characteristics and uses:

ARROWS MADE OF ALUMINUM

Both persons who shoot from a compound bow and those who use recurve bows may utilize these, making them excellent for beginners. You'll probably see a lot of aluminum arrows if you visit the range.

ARROWS MADE OF CARBON

These are quite popular with compound bow users and with hunters alike (although you can also use them with a recurve).

WOODEN ARROWS, the first arrow

You will grow to enjoy wooden arrows if you choose to take up traditional archery, and you will eventually discover how to build your own. That's really neat. Wooden arrows can be used with a recurve bow, but since they're more sensitive than aluminum and carbon, you shouldn't use them with a compound bow. As we already explained, compound bows drive arrows with a lot of power, and wooden arrows sometimes can't resist such pressure.

When discussing arrows, you'll often hear the following terms:

• Arrowhead.

This is the arrow's sharp tip at the front. Arrowheads come in a variety of weights (which is significant; we'll discuss it in a later post) and shapes, from very blunt to incredibly keen. You'll probably be utilizing "bullet point" arrows as a beginning archer because they have a sharp, but not overly sharp, tip. The arrowheads that bowhunters employ for game are referred to as "broadheads" from time to time. Most archery ranges forbid them because they are prohibitively risky and dangerously sharp.

• Shaft

The distance between the arrowhead and the fletching is known as the arrow's length.

• Fletching

These are the arrow's vanes, which can either be made of plastic or feathers (which is useful for target practice) (and this is good for hunting). The index vane is often the one vane on the arrow that is a different color than the other two vanes.

• **Nock**

The bifurcated end of the arrow that attaches to the bow string is at the back.

If you're looking for suggestions, we'd suggest the Carbon Express Maxima RED and the Easton Genesis V2 (both of which are feather-fleshed, reasonably durable, and excellent practice arrows) (these are very sturdy, have plastic vanes, are manufactured to a high degree of straightness, and can handle shots from high-poundage bows).

Easton Genesis V2 Arrows Black 1820 6 pk.
- Durable and economical
- Made from 7075 alloy
- The only arrow permitted in NASP competition

Carbon Express Maxima RED Fletched Carbon Arrows with Dynamic Spine Control and Blazer Vanes, 250 (.400 Spine), 6-Pack

• LAUNCHPAD PRECISION NOCK - Standard on all Maxima RED arrows and shafts, Launchpad Precision Nocks provide a controlled arrow release, improved shaft alignment, and increased accuracy shot after shot.
• DYNAMIC SPINE CONTROL - Patented high-tech carbon material construction that controls Dynamic Spine in a novel method to improve the flight of broadheads. Different types of carbon compounds are used by Maxima RED to restrict arrow flex to the RED ZONE.
• REAL STRAIGHTNESS - Laser verified to a remarkable 1/10,000 of an inch; straightness of +/- 0.0025 inches is a maximum measurement, not an average

Unbelievably, the making of arrows is one of the more challenging components of archery since various weights, measurement, and other procedures are used by different arrow manufacturers. But if you're eager to get started, check out our in-depth tutorial on arrows and how to select them.

HOW TO PURCHASE A BOW

A fun and simple process, purchasing a bow begins at an archery store with helpful, pleasant employees.
Tell them what kind of archery you want to pursue and your spending limit. Several bow recommendations will be made based on your preferences. The length of your draw, or how far you draw back the bowstring, will then be measured. The fun begins after that short measurement. You can try out the bows and select the one that feels the most comfortable.

Once you've decided on a bow, you can accessorize it. A sight, quiver, arrow rest, and release assistance are all necessary. To make your bow stand out, you can match the colors of your accessories. Your equipment can be further personalized with unique arrows and bowstrings.

The bow specialist at the archery store will put your attachments together, mount them, and adjust the bow so it is as comfortable and accurate as possible for you. The bow is then prepared for use! You can sign up for lessons and shoot it straight away.

ARROW BUYERS GUIDE

The choice of arrows is as important as the choice of bow. Let's learn about their components. The arrow's body is its shaft. The nock of the arrow attaches to the bowstring. The arrow is stabilized in flight by its fletchings, which are situated close to the nock. It should go without saying that the arrow's tip is what strikes the target.

ARROW SHAFT COMPONENTS

Most archers and bowhunters use carbon fiber as their preferred arrow material because of its strength and low weight. Carbon is incredibly resilient and, when bent, snaps back to its original form. That means that no matter how badly you abuse them, your arrows will remain straight.

*Safety Tip: Carbon arrows can tolerate tiny cracks during forceful hits to rock or metal. Manufacturers provide affordable carbon arrows that are perfect for starting archers. Check your arrow for damage if it misses the mark or strikes anything hard. Next, flex it while keeping an ear out for crackling sounds. Throw away or convert your broken or noisy arrow into an arrow pen.

Although less expensive, aluminum arrows are just as straight and consistent as carbon arrows. What is their main flaw? They don't last as long as carbon. From improper handling or harsh impacts, aluminum can bend. But aluminum is an excellent choice if you have a limited budget and take good care of your arrows.

Wooden arrows have been used by archers for thousands of years. They have been employed in battles like the Battle of Agincourt and in the pursuit of woolly mammoths. A well-oiled back quiver filled with hardwood arrows appeals to many archers' sense of nostalgia. They personify the romanticism and mysticism of archery.

Sadly, wooden arrows are less resilient than carbon or aluminum arrows and are more prone to warping. The traditional appearance and feel of wooden arrows, however, may offset the drawbacks for certain archers. Try using wooden arrows if you're a purist or wish to go back in time.

Fletchings

The two main types of fletchings are vanes and feathers, and they serve to stabilize the arrow while it is in flight.

Vanes are plastic fletchings. They are typically recommended for modern recurves and compound bows with high arrow rests. Because they are robust and watertight, vanes are widely used.

Feathers are a great choice when you need your arrows to be as responsive and solid as possible. Because of this, traditional archers and many competitive archers choose feathers for indoor competitions. The fletching of an arrow that is fired from a recurve or longbow makes contact with the bow. Due to their flexibility, feathers flatten down when they come into contact with a bow and don't interfere with arrow flight. Although powders and sprays can make feathers water-resistant, they are not waterproof.

Additionally, think about the length and style of your fletchings. In general, firing outside and at a greater distance benefits from a shorter, low-profile vane since it lessens drag and wind drift. For indoor or close-range outdoor archery, a longer vane with a higher profile is preferable.

Arrow spine

The spine is a measurement of the flex or bend of an arrow. The spine number of the arrow can be found on its label. 350, 400, 500, and 600 are a few instances. The flex of the arrow increases with the number. Keep using the arrow spine you've chosen once you've found one that works for your bow. The only exception is if you modify your bow, such raising the draw weight. A stiffer arrow is required for a bow with a heavy draw weight, and a more flexible arrow is required for a bow with a lighter draw weight.

Arrow spine is influenced by numerous factors, including bow design, arrow length, and point weight. When choosing your arrow shafts, the specialists at your local archery shop take these things into account.

Nock fit

The fit between your bowstring and arrow nock is crucial but frequently disregarded. The arrow releases from the bowstring with a little tap once the perfect fit snaps audibly onto it. If your nock won't neatly release from the string, it may be overly tight, which may reduce accuracy. It's dangerous if your nock is too loose since it could cause the arrow to come off the string as you draw.

Arrow length

From the back of the tip to the throat of the nock is the traditional measurement for arrow length. Your arrow length is influenced by the draw length and spine of your arrow. Your arrow would be around 27 inches long if your draw length is 28 inches and you want it to terminate at the front of the riser. However, if you need to weaken the arrow's spine, you can make your arrow longer. Don't make your arrows too short for safety's sake. Your arrows are precisely measured by the expert at your local archery shop.

When selecting arrows, there are numerous factors to consider. The experience at archery shops makes the process simple if you're feeling overwhelmed. Just let the technician know your spending limit, the details of your bow, and the kind of shooting you like to do (field, 3D, indoor or target).

SELECT THE PROPER ARROWHEADS

- Make your own or purchase ready-made arrows, but make sure to pick arrows with the appropriate heads for the task. Use only broadheads, judo or blunt heads when hunting small game, target or bullet arrowheads while practicing archery, and bowfishing arrowheads when fishing.

- Never use arrowheads for a purpose other than what they were designed for; otherwise, they may become dull or broken and useless just when you need them. Because of safety concerns, the majority of store-bought broadheads aren't very sharp when you buy them; you'll need to sharpen them before using.
- For hunting, you should utilize arrowheads with broadheads.

They can be as sharp as surgical instruments and come in a variety of shapes that are intended to inflict deadly wounds. Use caution when touching them.

Final Remarks

The dependable bow and arrow is the most effective non-powder projectile weapon in terms of dependability, ease of use, upkeep, and effectiveness. You'll need to put a lot of effort into honing and maintaining this talent as a component of your arsenal of survival techniques. Don't wait to use your bow if you already have one for "just in case" scenarios. Practice using it so you are comfortable with how it functions and feels. Since the day may come when you'll need this talent to hunt for food or perhaps battle for your life, practice until firing your bow and successfully hitting a target becomes an almost instinctual and natural activity for you.

WHERE TO BUY BOW AND ARROWS

Pro shops can be found all across the United States and Canada, and the majority of them stock thousands of different archery goods. Sadly, some pro shops employ salesmen who have no idea what they're talking about and are only there to attempt to sell you something. However, some pro shops use salespeople who do know what they're talking about. Before visiting a pro shop, it's a good idea to conduct some research about archery so you can differentiate a knowledgeable salesperson from one who doesn't know his head from a hole in the ground. Online retailers also offer archery equipment. Although there are quite a few "big-name" online retailers that sell archery gear, you can also buy from many incredibly specialized archery and bowhunting outfitters. Given that there are literally thousands of firms that produce archery products and that you might eventually wish to purchase a product from one you've never heard of, the reviews on these websites can be really helpful.

You can choose between professional shops and online retailers. You can merely visit the range if you don't feel ready to purchase a bow, though have we talked about ranges yet? No? You can hire bows and arrows there; we'll get to it in a moment. That's a GREAT alternative for beginners because it can be challenging to determine the right size bow, type of arrows, etc. When you arrive at the range, they will provide you with everything you need, so you can dive right in.

CHAPTER 4

SOME BASIC RULES YOU SHOULD KNOW ABOUT ARCHERY

Adults and children practice archery all around the world, and provided everyone takes the necessary safety precautions, it can be a highly entertaining and secure past hour.

In light of this, there are a few guidelines you'll want to remember at all times. Among others, they consist of...

- Always abide by the regulations in your area. You must learn and abide by the regulations that govern your range.
- Always use proper form when shooting. Archery is a repetitive sport; if you aim incorrectly, you run the risk of long-term injury;
- Put On Appropriate Clothes. In other words, AVOID wearing anything that might get in the way of your shot and hurt you or someone else. Open-toed shoes, loose jewelry, loose

attire, and long hair need to be tied back are all no-nos;

- Wear the proper protective equipment. The phrase "damaged gear is dangerous gear" is used to describe a variety of items, including arm protectors, bow releases, and helmets when playing Archery Tag. Avoid shooting broken or damaged arrows, and always examine your bow to make sure it's in great condition;
- Don't ever dry fire a bow. Another major no-no is "dry firing," which is pulling back the bow string and releasing it without an arrow. This puts you and the bow in danger and damages the bow, sending pieces flying around that can be sharp.
- Aim Only at the Target. Always aim at the target and never point the bow—drawn or not—at anything you wouldn't want to hit. Always operate under the assumption that you will hit what you shoot at.

You've got a Great Start. You now are aware of the two primary types of bows, some basic information about arrows, the advantages of a range, and resources where you may learn more as your skills advance. You should be thrilled because everything are going well thus far.

TIPS FOR ALL ARCHERS ON HOW TO PICK A BOW SIGHT

Are you trying to find your first bow sight? Or do you want to replace the sight on your bow with a new, more stunning one? When deciding which bow sights are best for your bow, there are a lot of aspects to consider, and it can be easy to become a little overwhelmed by the information. Depending on the kind of bow you shoot, the kinds of archery you enjoy, and your particular shooting style, you'll want a different kind of sight. You'll find all the crucial information on this page that you need to choose the ideal sight for you.

COMPARISON OF SINGLE AND MULTI-PIN SIGHTS

The first thing to decide is whether you want a fixed pin multi pin sight or a single pin adjustable sight. As they will excel at various forms of archery and with various purposes, they each have their own special benefits.

One aiming pin is present with single pin sights, and it can be "dialed in" to a certain range or distance. So, for instance: You just need to change the dial for the specified yardage and you're ready to shoot if you wish to aim at a target that is 30 yards away. With each shot, you must compensate for any future range.

Multi-pinned sights have fixed pins that are typically incapable of any field adjustment at all. Before using your bow sight, you must sight it in over multiple sessions at a practice range. There are a few multi-pinned sights that can be altered while you're in the field, but they are often quite pricey right now. If you're wanting to purchase one of these kinds of sights, plan to pay somewhat more.

Multiple aiming pins, each set for a different distance, are present in multi pin sights. As an illustration A multi pin sight may be configured for distances of 20, 30, and 40 yards, respectively.

Multi-pin sights are typically used by hunters because they allow for quick and simple range adjustments in the event that the target moves closer or farther away from you. A deer might be 20 yards away from you when you shoot with the 20 yard pin, but then it might suddenly dash to a distance of 40 yards. You only need to change your aim to point at the 40-yard pin. This enables fast adjustments while the bow is still pulled for various ranges. That can also aid you when you're hunting since if you have to move to let the bow draw back in, correct the sight, and then pull the bow back again, the deer can very well notice you.

Despite this, many archers continue to hunt with single pin sights; in fact, some prefer them to multi pin sights since they provide a much clearer sight picture.

There are various 3 pin, 5 pin, and 7 pin sights available on the market today, so if you want to go with one, you have a lot of options.

As I indicated above, the many archery disciplines you practice will frequently determine the kind of sight you wish to use.

Single Pin Sights

Field and target archery both benefit greatly from single pin sights. In actuality, these are both of their preferred sites. For 3D archery, single pin sights are also excellent. There's really no need for more than three pins at once when using 3D archery, but I find that both single pin and (less pinned) multi pin sights can be entertaining.

Multi Pin Sights

You should probably at least take a look at a few multi pin sights if hunting is your main interest. They're essentially created just for hunting, and multi pin sights are now much more reasonably priced than they were a few years ago. A multi pin sight might be the best option if you plan to shoot a combination of hunting and 3D archery. Remember that multi-pin sights with 7 or more pins are available, and more isn't always better.

On the other hand, adding more pins will result in a cluttered view of your site. Many an archer has cursed in the woods after missing a deer because of a cluttered sight picture or shooting at the wrong target.

Don't completely disregard single pin sights for hunting. It might be worthwhile to take one on a few hunts if you know someone who will let you borrow one to determine whether you prefer it to a multi-pin sight or not.

FOR BEGINNER ARCHERS

I would strongly advise starting with either a single pin sight or a three pinned multi pin sight if you are somewhat new to archery, depending on which seems appropriate for the types of archery that you intend to shoot.

In conclusion: Field and target archers ought to begin with a single pin sight. While 3D archers can use whichever one they like, hunters should choose a multi pin sight.

SIZE OF PINS

Multi-pin sights also have a variety of sized aiming pins. Ten thousandths of an inch is used to measure pin sizes, with the most popular values being .029, .019, and .010, respectively. Smaller pins will help you place the arrow precisely where you want it to be and will maintain your sight picture clearer and more accurate. They are also much better for long-range shooting because they hide less of the target that you are aiming at.

Larger pins are preferable for low light settings overall since they will capture more light. Larger pins will also clog up your field of vision. When deciding which type to utilize, there is always a trade-off because each has benefits and drawbacks of its own.

There is a technique to somewhat balance this and perhaps achieve the best of both worlds:

For your initial, shorter-range pins, you can use bigger diameter fibers; for your later, longer-range pins, you can use smaller diameter fibers.

For larger pins, use fibers up to .050 inches, and for smaller, long-range pins, use the smallest size possible—.010 inches.

These figures should not be interpreted as dictating exactly what you must do. Though many archers will find themselves at ease with various settings, it's not a big deal. This is merely intended to be a jumping off point to assist you in locating your ideal configuration. A lot of archers simply stick to using .019 pins, which are now the standard pin size for many archers.

If there is an archery shop nearby, try out a few different sights with various pin sizes if you can. If there isn't one nearby, ask your friends or other 3D club shooters if they would allow you use theirs.

FIBER OPTICS

Fiber optics are made into many sights. These work well in dimly lit areas because they illuminate the pointing pins, making them easily visible.

Generally speaking, a sight will have more light in it the more fiber it contains. Fiber optics are typically used by hunters in the early morning or when shooting after sunset. Fiber optics are basically only a problem for hunters because most other forms of archery are rarely used in low-light situations.

SIGHT LIGHTS

Sight lights, which are battery-operated lights that shine into the sight and allow you to see the pointing pins in the dark, are another feature of some sights that particularly aids hunters. Although they are often prohibited from use, they can be helpful to hunters who hunt at dawn or dark. In fact, many states now forbid hunters from using any form of technological device linked to their bow. Since sight lights are regarded as electronic devices, the same regulations apply to them.

Additionally, hunting is prohibited in several states either before or after the sun rises. Before you go hunting, be sure you are abiding by any local laws by checking them.

BUBBLE LEVELS

A bubble level, a little plastic vile filled with colored alcohol and used to help level your shots, is now a common feature on many modern sights. The bubble will indicate whether you're tilting your photo too much to the right or left, same to how the level hardware tool does. In order to be used in cold weather, they are typically filled with either alcohol or other colored liquids that won't freeze. To prevent them from shooting to the side or the other, compound archers are really the only ones who ever need these.

Recurve shooters won't need to rely as heavily on bubble levels as compound archers because many recurve archers like to shoot their bow with only a slight tilt while remaining on target.

GANG ADJUSTMENTS

Some sights have a function that enables you to simultaneously adjust all of your aiming pins. You may change them all from one location rather than having to shoot at various yardages for each unique aiming pin one at a time.

Unless you discover that you continually need to adjust your sight for both windage and elevation, the majority of archers won't find that they need this capability. Make sure the sight you choose to purchase allows you to adjust the aiming pins without the use of a special wrench if it requires gang adjustments. While most individuals don't need them, some archers may benefit from such changes to help them avoid occasional side-to-side misses. Don't worry if your sight doesn't have this feature if you're new at archery.

SEVERAL GENERAL HINTS

The bar that supports the sight and fastens it to the bow is known as a sight bar. The size and effectiveness of the sight bar are two considerations you should address when comparing various bow sights.

Smaller or shorter sight bars make it simpler to move around in the woods without becoming tangled in tree limbs and brush, even though larger sight bars often are a little more accurate.

How reliable is the sight bar as well? Although sights with lower-quality sight bars are typically less expensive, you are essentially giving up solid construction in exchange for the reduced cost. A nice, durable metal sight bar will outperform a subpar plastic one and survive longer.

Micro-adjustment

Some of the more expensive bow sights have the ability for in-field micro-adjustment. With the use of no special instruments, this function enables archers to modify the pins in their sight wherever they are. While having the ability to change your sight picture whenever you want is excellent, doing so would require a significant rise in the sight's price. You must decide whether it is worthwhile to pay a significant premium for this luxury. The pin locations are typically locked in place by a simple locking screw on most of these sights. You can adjust the aiming pin placements and the sight's windage (to the left and right) by loosening this.

Without a doubt, this is a cool feature to have on any bow sight, but is the additional cost justified? It's not, in my view.

You shouldn't have to do this while you're in the field if you take the time to sight in your bow properly. You shouldn't have to worry about whether or not your sight has this feature for the time being, especially if you're new to archery. If you ultimately determine that you absolutely cannot function without micro-adjustment, you can always update your sight.

I sincerely hope that this tutorial has given you some insight into what to specifically consider when selecting a new bow sight. When you are comparing prices for bow sights, keep in mind the things I have showed you to look for and avoid. Have fun shooting and good luck with your purchases.

Printed in Great Britain
by Amazon

Printed in Great Britain
by Amazon